SLEEPYTIME RHYME

Remy Charlip

GREENWILLOW BOOKS · NEW YORK

FOR MY FATHER, MAX, AND MY SON, JULES

I WOULD LIKE TO THANK ERIC DEKKER FOR HIS HELP AND SUPPORT.

WATERCOLOR WASHES ON ARCHES PAPER WERE USED FOR THE FULL-COLOR ART.
THE TEXT TYPE IS ALBERTUS.

PRINTED IN SINGAPORE BY TIEN WAH PRESS
FIRST EDITION
10 9 8 7 6 5 4 3 2

LIBRARY OF CONGRESS CATALOGING-IN-PUBLICATION DATA

CHARLIP, REMY.
SLEEPYTIME RHYME / BY REMY CHARLIP.
    P.   CM.
SUMMARY: ILLUSTRATIONS AND RHYMING TEXT CONVEY A MOTHER'S LOVE FOR HER CHILD.
ISBN 0-688-16271-1 (TRADE).   ISBN 0-688-16272-X (LIB. BDG.)
[1. MOTHER AND CHILD–FICTION.   2. BABIES–FICTION.   3. STORIES IN RHYME.]
I. TITLE.   PZ8.3.C386SI   1999   [E]–DC21   98-41040   CIP   AC

I LOVE YOU.
I THINK
YOU'RE GRAND.
THERE'S NONE
LIKE YOU
IN ALL THE LAND.

I LOVE
YOUR HAIR,
YOUR HEAD,
YOUR CHIN,
YOUR NECK,
EACH EAR,
BOTH CHEEKS,
YOUR SKIN.

YOUR SPECIAL
FACE,
YOUR EYES,
YOUR MOUTH.
I LOVE
YOUR KNEES,
YOUR NORTH,
YOUR SOUTH.

I LOVE
YOUR HANDS,
YOUR TEETH,
YOUR NOSE,
YOUR ANKLES,
FEET,
AND ALL
TEN TOES.

I LOVE
YOUR WEST,
YOUR EAST,
YOUR CHEST.
IT'S HARD
TO SAY
WHAT I
LOVE BEST.

YOUR ARMS?
YOUR LEGS?
YOUR HIPS?
YOUR LIPS?
I EVEN
LOVE
YOUR
FINGERTIPS.

I LOVE YOU,
EACH
AND EVERY
PART . . .
YES,
ALL OF YOU,
WITH ALL
MY HEART.

I LOVE YOU
HERE,
AND THERE,
AND HERE.
I LOVE TO
HUG YOU,
HOLD YOU
NEAR.

IN ALL
THE LAND
THERE'S NONE
LIKE YOU.
YOU'RE VERY GRAND . . .

I DO LOVE YOU.

Remy Charlip

KNEW HE WANTED TO BE INVOLVED WITH
PICTURE BOOKS WHEN HE GRADUATED
FROM COOPER UNION IN 1949. HE SAYS
HE WAS FORTUNATE TO HAVE BEGUN HIS
CAREER WITH TWO BRILLIANT PICTURE
BOOK PIONEERS: MARGARET WISE BROWN
(THE DEAD BIRD AND DAVID'S LITTLE INDIAN)
AND RUTH KRAUSS (A MOON OR A BUTTON).
SINCE THEN HE HAS COLLABORATED WITH
MANY TALENTED AUTHORS AS WELL AS
WRITTEN AND ILLUSTRATED SUCH MODERN
CLASSICS AS THIRTEEN, ARM IN ARM, AND
FORTUNATELY. IN ADDITION, MR. CHARLIP
HAS ACTED IN AND WRITTEN PLAYS,
CHOREOGRAPHED AND PERFORMED DANCES,
AND DESIGNED SETS AND COSTUMES.
HE LIVES IN SAN FRANCISCO, CALIFORNIA.
(www.remycharlip.com)